THE SOLAR SYSTEM FOR SMARTYPANTS

Anushka Ravishankar
ILLUSTRATED BY
Pia Alizé Hazarika

duckbill

An imprint of Penguin Random House

DUCKBILL BOOKS

USA | Canada | UK | Ireland | Australia
New Zealand | India | South Africa | China

Duckbill Books is part of the Penguin Random House group of companies
whose addresses can be found at global.penguinrandomhouse.com

Published by
Penguin Random House India Pvt. Ltd
4th Floor, Capital Tower 1, MG Road,
Gurugram 122 002, Haryana, India

Penguin
Random House
India

First published in Duckbill Books by
Penguin Random House India 2022

10 9 8 7 6 5 4 3 2 1

This is a work of non-fiction. The views and opinions expressed in this book are the
author's own and the facts are as reported by her which have been verified to the extent
possible, and the publishers are not in any way liable for the same.

ISBN 9780143454137

Typeset in ArcherPro by DiTech Publishing Services Pvt. Ltd
Printed at Aarvee Promotions, India

www.penguin.co.in

The
SOLAR SYSTEM
consists of the sun, and all the
bodies bound to it by gravity,
including the planets and their
moons, dwarf planets, asteroids,
comets and meteoroids.

The sun is the star at the centre of our solar system.

YES, IT IS A STAR.
NO, YOU CAN'T SEE IT AT NIGHT.
NO, IT DOESN'T TWINKLE.
NO, IT'S NOT LIKE A DIAMOND IN THE SKY. IT IS STILL A STAR.

The solar system is made up of the sun, which is at the centre, the planets and many other smaller bodies, which go around the sun.

GRAAAAR
NOT THAT KIND OF BODY.
I WAS NOT TRYING TO SCARE YOU.
OKAY, NOT BODIES, THINGS!

The smaller things are dwarf planets, moons, asteroids, comets and meteoroids.

We call it the solar system because the sun is also known as Sol, which comes from the Latin word for sun—solis. So anything to do with the sun is called 'solar'.

NO, NO ONE CALLS IT THE SUNAR SYSTEM.
YOU CAN CALL IT THAT IF YOU LIKE, BUT NOBODY WILL KNOW WHAT YOU'RE TALKING ABOUT.

The planets go around the sun. The invisible path on which a planet travels is called an **orbit**.

The gravity of the sun makes the planets go around it in a fixed orbit.

REMEMBER WE LEARNT ABOUT GRAVITY?*

NO, I DON'T WANT YOU TO TELL ME ALL ABOUT GRAVITY NOW.

YES, OKAY, YOU REMEMBER EVERYTHING.

*GRAVITY FOR SMARTYPANTS

The time taken by a planet
to spin around fully is a day.
This is called **rotation**.

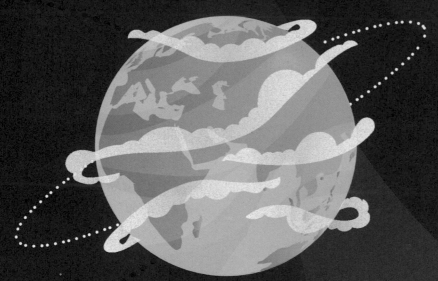

The time taken by a planet
to go around the sun is a year.
This is called **revolution**.

YES, IF YOU KEEP SPINNING YOU WILL FALL DOWN.
NO, PLANETS DON'T FALL DOWN. THAT'S ALSO BECAUSE OF THE GRAVITY OF THE SUN.
THUNK

The planet closest to the sun is Mercury. It is the smallest planet in our solar system. The sunlight on Mercury is much brighter than on Earth.

Mercury takes only 88 Earth days to go around the sun. So one year on Mercury is 88 days, while one year on Earth is 365 Earth days.

1 EARTH YEAR = ABOUT 4 MERCURY YEARS

MERCURY

DISTANCE FROM THE SUN = 57.9 MILLION KM

MERCURY DAY = 59 EARTH DAYS

MERCURY YEAR = 88 EARTH DAYS

NUMBER OF MOONS = 0

HOW WILL YOUR BIRTHDAY COME FOUR TIMES A YEAR ON MERCURY?
NO, IT WON'T.
NO, YOU CAN'T GO LIVE ON MERCURY.
NO, I WON'T BUY YOU A BIRTHDAY GIFT FOUR TIMES A YEAR.
NO, I WON'T.

Venus is the second planet from the sun, but it is the hottest planet in the solar system. It is so hot that even lead would melt on it.

On Venus, the sun rises in the west and sets in the east. This is because Venus spins from east to west.

PHEW

VENUS

DISTANCE FROM THE SUN = 108.2 MILLION KM

VENUS DAY = 243 EARTH DAYS

VENUS YEAR = 225 EARTH DAYS

NUMBER OF MOONS = 0

No, IF YOU SPIN FROM EAST TO WEST, YOU WON'T SEE THE SUN RISE IN THE WEST.
BECAUSE YOU'RE ON EARTH, AND EARTH SPINS FROM WEST TO EAST.
OKAY, YOU CAN TRY IT.

Earth is the third planet from the sun. It is the only planet in the solar system which has water on its surface. It is also the only planet we know of which has living things on it.

EARTH

DISTANCE FROM THE SUN = 149.6 MILLION KM
EARTH DAY = 24 HOURS
EARTH YEAR = 365 EARTH DAYS
NUMBER OF MOONS = 1

YES, LIKE YOU.
YES, LIKE ME.
YES, LIKE THAT BEE.
YES, LIKE THAT PLANT.
OKAY, YOU GET THE IDEA.
ENOUGH!

Mars is the fourth planet from the sun.

It is much smaller than Earth. It looks red because it has red soil. That's why it is called the Red Planet.

MARS

DISTANCE FROM THE SUN = 227.9 MILLION KM
MARS DAY = 24 EARTH HOURS
MARS YEAR = 687 EARTH DAYS
NUMBER OF MOONS = 2

Mars is a cold, rocky and dusty planet.

NO, MY ROOM IS NOT LIKE MARS. I DUSTED IT JUST A FEW DAYS AGO!

NO, NO ONE NEEDS TO DUST MARS. IT'S NOT THAT KIND OF DUSTY!

Jupiter is the fifth planet from the sun.
It is the biggest planet in the solar system.

If you look at Jupiter through a telescope,
you will see the Great Red Spot.

This spot is actually a storm that has been
going on for 300 years.

JUPITER

DISTANCE FROM THE SUN = 778.3 MILLION KM

JUPITER DAY = 10 EARTH HOURS

JUPITER YEAR = 12 EARTH YEARS

NUMBER OF MOONS = MORE THAN 75

Some of Jupiter's 75 moons have oceans beneath their surface. There might be life in these oceans.

THERE MAY BE FISH, I DON'T KNOW.

NO, I CAN'T TAKE YOU TO ONE OF JUPITER'S MOONS.

NO!

Saturn is the sixth planet from the sun. It is the second biggest planet in the solar system. It is mostly made up of gas.

Saturn has seven beautiful rings around it.

SATURN

DISTANCE FROM THE SUN = 1,427.0 MILLION KM

SATURN DAY = 10.7 EARTH HOURS

SATURN YEAR = 29 EARTH YEARS

NUMBER OF MOONS = 82

(53 KNOWN AND 29 TO BE CONFIRMED)

NO, THEY'RE NOT MADE UP OF DIAMONDS. NOR RUBIES. NOR TOPAZ. THEY'RE MADE OF ROCKS AND ICE.

YES, YOUR COLLAR IS PRETTIER THAN THE RINGS OF SATURN.
UM, THEY'RE NOT DIAMONDS.
MRRRRRRR
I NEVER SAID THEY WERE!

Uranus is the seventh planet from the sun.

It is a gaseous planet. It has thirteen rings around it, some dark, some colourful.

Like Venus, it rotates from east to west. But it rotates on its side.

YES, I KNOW YOU CAN ROTATE ON YOUR SIDE, AND YOU ALSO HAVE A LOT OF GAS.

UGH. NOT NOW, PLEASE.

NO, I WON'T CHANGE YOUR NAME TO URANUS.

Neptune is the eighth and last planet in our solar system. It is an icy planet because it is so far away from the sun. The heat of the sun does not reach it, so it is dark and cold.

It has five main rings and some half-rings made of dust rocks.

NEPTUNE
DISTANCE FROM THE SUN = 4,497.1 MILLION KM
NEPTUNE DAY = 16 EARTH HOURS
NEPTUNE YEAR = 165 EARTH YEARS
NUMBER OF MOONS = 14 KNOWN
YOU DON'T HAVE TO LIKE NEPTUNE.
OKAY, WE WON'T GO THERE.

Pluto used to be called the ninth planet of the solar system. But then astronomers found out that it is not a planet but a dwarf planet.

PLUTO

DISTANCE FROM THE SUN: 5,913 MILLION KM
PLUTO DAY = 6 EARTH DAYS
PLUTO YEAR = 248 EARTH YEARS
NUMBER OF MOONS = 5

Oi!!

Pluto has blue skies, high mountains and red snow.

YES, RED SNOW MUST BE PRETTY.

NO, WE CAN'T GO THERE, BECAUSE IT IS TOO COLD. NOTHING LIVES THERE.

NO, NOT EVEN FISH.

FINE, WE WON'T GO TO PLUTO.

There's an easy way to remember the planets in order.

My	Mercury
Very	Venus
Educated	Earth
Mother	Mars
Just	Jupiter
Served	Saturn
Us	Uranus
Nine	Neptune
Pizzas	Pluto

I CAN'T HELP IT IF YOU DON'T LIKE PIZZA.
THAT'S TRUE, PLUTO IS NOT A PLANET.
OKAY, YOU MAKE UP ONE, THEN.

IT'S HARDER TO REMEMBER THE NAMES OF THESE FISH THAN THE NAMES OF THE PLANETS!
MAYBE NOT FOR YOU, BUT FOR MOST HUMANS.
YOU MAY NOT CARE, BUT I DO.

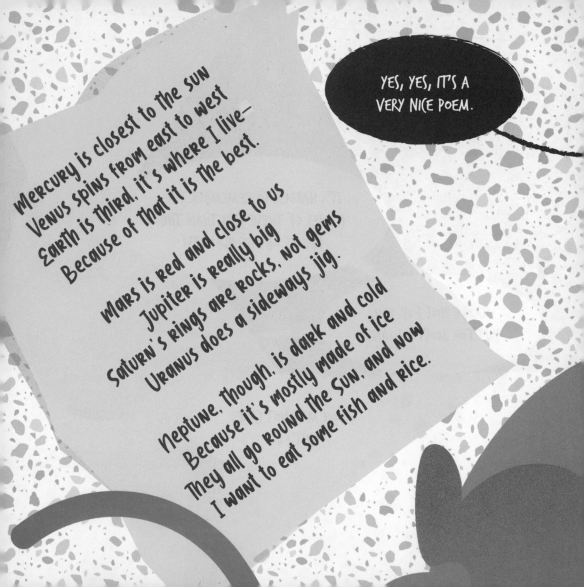

NO, NO FISH AND RICE FOR YOU. IT'S NOT LUNCHTIME YET.
OKAY, YOU'LL GET A TREAT.
JUST ONE.
NO, JUST ONE.
YES, SMARTYPANTS, YOU KNOW ALL ABOUT THE SOLAR SYSTEM NOW.

Anushka Ravishankar likes science, cats and books, not necessarily in that order. So she decided to write a book to explain science to a cat. The cat doesn't always get the point, but she hopes her readers will.

Pia Alizé Hazarika is an illustrator primarily interested in comics and visual narratives.

Her independent/collaborative work has been published by Penguin Random House India (*The PAO Anthology*), COMIX INDIA, Manta Ray Comics, The Pulpocracy, Captain Bijli Comics, Yoda Press, Zubaan Books and the Khoj Artists Collective. She runs PIG Studio, an illustration-driven space, based out of New Delhi.

Her handle on Instagram is @_PigStudio_